The

Jesus in the Beginning

Creation & Primeval History

Genesis 1–11

2

The amazing story of . . .

Jesus in the Beginning

*Creation &
Primeval History*

Genesis 1–11

'If you believed Moses, you would believe Me; because he wrote about Me.' **John 5:46**

In the Beginning, the Bible doesn't just speak about Creation and the birth of civilization, Moses wrote about Jesus from the very first verse.

Published by PUSH Publishing 2017

www.pushpublishing.co.uk

in partnership with Jesus Centred Bible

office@jesuscentred.org

www.jesuscentred.org

Scripture quotations are based on the World English
Bible (WEB) which is in the public domain.
The WEB is a 1997 revision of the American Standard
Version of 1901.

A catalogue record for this book is
available from the British Library

ISBN-13: 978-0-9933445-5-8

Printed and bound in Great Britain by Cambrian Printers

Cover design by Joseph Laycock

Contents

Dedication

Special Thanks To:

Georgian Banov, who took a chance in supporting me a few years back when I most needed it. It was a small but crucial step on the journey that has produced this series of books.

And thanks to the others who have become partners along the way too. In particular I want to mention: Peter David Aston, Sally Bennett, Colin Burns, Anne Campbell, Barbara Dingle, Howard Dwyer, Helen Gray, Colin Green, Leah Jenkin, Joan Johnson, Mark and Ruth Middleton and Ibukin Shorinwa.

Teaching and writing is so much more fun when you can share it as it happens!

Introduction

The Rabbis call Genesis, 'In The Beginning' from its first word, *b-rashyth /* בראשת. But they saw the book as being structured around a different Hebrew word, *toledot /* תולדות, which means 'generations'. The phrase, 'These are the generations of . . .' breaks Genesis into ten sections (see *Appendix*) and, because the Greek word for 'generations' is γενεσεως / *geneseos*, the first book of the Old Testament has come to us as 'The Book of Genesis', 'The Book of Generations'.

But these sections, defined by the word 'Genesis', vary hugely in length and surprisingly there is no specific 'generations' section for Abraham. So modern commentators retain the name Genesis for the book, but not its structure; they now break the book into two main sections with an introduction.

Introduction	**Genesis 1:1 – 2:3**	Creation
Section 1	**Genesis 2:4 – 11:32**	Primeval History
Section 2	**Genesis 12:1 – 50:26**	Patriarchs

The next book in the series, *Volume 3: Jesus in the Fathers – Patriarchs & Promises*, will cover **Genesis 12 – 50**.

This book, *Volume 2*, will unpack **Genesis 1 – 11** in two parts: *Creation* and *Primeval History*.

Creation

The first half of this volume will explore the connection between Christ and Creation. But to do this we will consider all of **Genesis 1 – 11** along with other Creation passages from the Old and New Testament. This half of the volume is theologically a bit deeper than the second half.

Primeval History

The second half of this volume will follow the events and people that came before Abraham. There are some remarkable references to Jesus in these stories, but they are a bit more self-contained and tied to moments in history than the symbols and memes of the Creation section of Genesis.

With both sections, take the time to understand the truth you're exploring: look up the references and try reading them in different Bibles; make your own notes to record your own thoughts and cross-references; and remember that some truths are better felt than they are systematised.

Even so I would still encourage you to develop a system to organise and annotate what you see, learn and feel and to start transferring notes to your own Bible. Or you can adopt and adapt my system (see below). A system helps you build 'precept upon precept, line upon line . . .' **Isaiah 28:10**. With time you'll find the Old Testament has become as Jesus-centred as the New.

Using these notes

These books have been written to reflect the six streams of Christo-centric revelation that I've settled on over the years. In my Bible, these streams are colour-coded but each stream also has an icon, because colour isn't always possible. And there is a seventh icon too, used to highlight when a revelation is a bit more cryptic.

You will find these icons scattered through this book to highlight an aspect of the truth being explored. I've not always explained why a particular paragraph of this book is connected to a specific icon and its stream of revelation, but you should be able to work out why for yourself.

Prophecy: Predictive, Ecstatic and Formative

 Typology: Models, Titles, People and Events

 Teaching: Used by Jesus / Gospels

 Jesus' Household: The Family Tree

 Trinity and Divinity: Jesus as God / God as a Plurality

 Christophanies: God in visible form

 Cryptic: Hidden in the Hebrew

Part 1

Creation

Creation

In the Beginning . . .

I n 1968, Apollo 8 circled the moon. As it emerged from radio silence behind Earth's silvery sibling, an estimated half-billion people watched a grainy image of our home planet rising over a lunar horizon on their TV screens; and then they heard the voice of astronaut William Anders:

> We are now approaching lunar sunrise, and for all the people back on Earth, the crew of Apollo 8 has a message that we would like to send to you, 'In the Beginning God created the heavens and the earth . . . '

Between them the three astronauts William, Jim Lovell and Frank Borman read the first ten verses of Genesis.

Words written in antiquity beautifully complemented the moment humanity's view of itself and its home planet changed. And then because it was December 24, Frank Borman signed off on behalf of the crew by wishing the world a 'Merry Christmas'.

The Old Testament starts with Creation, the New Testament starts with Christmas. But 'The Book of Genesis' is actually the New Testament's opening phrase:

The Book of Genesis (**the generations**) of Jesus
... **Matthew 1:1**

It is as though Matthew saw his Gospel as a new section to God's first book. He goes on to describe the events of the first Christmas when, as his fellow Gospel writer John put it, 'the Word became flesh and lived among us', **John 1:1**; the Creator became Creation, there was something new under the sun.

John starts his Gospel with the other title for Genesis: *b-rashyth* / בראשת: 'In the beginning . . .', but changes what follows because when 'God created', 'the Word' already 'was'.

The apostle John was Jesus' cousin. John's mother was Mary's sister, so John knew Jesus better than most and John saw Jesus in Genesis. He understood that Moses wrote about Jesus from his opening sentence. John records Philip's words:

> We have found Him, of whom Moses in the law, and the prophets, wrote ... **John 1:45**

The first eleven chapters of Genesis contain a section that theologians call the 'Proto-Evangelium' or the 'Primitive Gospel'. They also speak about Jesus' birth and life, the Cross and the resurrection and even about His return at the end of the age. In them we find ideas taught by Jesus;

prophecies plain and hidden, models and images, the Trinity and more. But let's start: 'In the beginning . . .' with 'the Word', **John 1:1**.

Ⓟ The Word AT the Beginning

When the apostle John read the first verse of the Bible he noticed something we don't. It was a little word, the Hebrew word *AT*, (את in Assyrian script, or ＋𝒳 in the original Hebrew pictograms – see the Alphabet table in the *Appendix* of *Volume 1: Jesus in the Old Testament*). In Hebrew, **Genesis 1:1** reads (right to left):

בראשית ברא אלהים את השמים ואת הארץ

h-eretz w-at h-shmim at Elohim bara b-rashyth

the earth   the heavens   created

and (AT)   *AT*   God / Elohim   In the beginning

AT joins 'God' / *Elohim* to His Creation. But *AT* doesn't get translated into English or Greek, though it is the most common word in the Hebrew Bible. It appears over 7000 times in its purest form and over 9000 times when you allow its variants – which is as often as *Elohim* / 'God' (2500+)

and *YHWH* / 'Lord' (6500+) put together. Even in John's day *AT* was often omitted when the Hebrew scriptures were read out loud, it seemed such an unimportant word. But John saw it was there and drew attention to it as the *'The Word'*, because 'AT' is a cryptic title for Jesus.

 In *Volume 1: Jesus in the Old Testament* we saw that *AT* is made up of the first and last letters of the Hebrew alphabet, Aleph-א and Tav-ת, and in John's final book, **Revelation**, Jesus speaking to John says in the Bible's last message:

> I am the Alpha and the Omega, the first and the last, the beginning and the end.
> **Revelation 22:13** (see also **1:8,11** and **21:6**)

John recounts this vision in Greek, so he uses the first and last letters of that alphabet, Alpha-α and Omega-ω, but it is likely that Jesus would have spoken to him in Hebrew or Aramaic, just as He did with Paul, **Acts 26:14**. In this case Jesus would have explicitly said, '*I am the Aleph-א and the Tav-ת*', confirming the connection John had already made in the introduction to his Gospel.

AT is the hidden word that *'was God'* and *'was with God'* in **Genesis 1:1**. It is the centrepiece of the seven-word sentence that opens up the Bible, and it extends the name *Elohim*.

Elohim / אלהים is the plural form of the noun *Eloah*

/ אלוה, 'supreme god' which is the emphatic form of *El*, meaning simply 'god' or 'power'. As God's title, the plural *Elohim* is used in the Bible with singular verbs. The only exception to this rule is when the sentence also includes a plural pronoun such as 'us', 'our' or 'we'. For instance in **Genesis 1:26**:

> Then *Elohim* (plural) said (singular) '*Let Us* make (plural) mankind in *Our* image.

 Elohim is a plural unity, it implies the Trinity so perhaps we should translate it as 'Multi-God', 'Plural-God' or 'Manifold-God'.

If we expand the phrase *Elohim AT* with the symbolic meanings of *AT* as we unpacked them in *Volume 1: Jesus in the Old Testament*, **Genesis 1:1** reads:

> In the beginning Multi-God-AT [first-and-last, binding-covenant, wounded-God, the-biggest-sacrifice-on-a-cross] created the heavens and the earth.

This is a good point to transfer some notes into your Bible

The Logic of God

John knew that most of his Greek Bible-reading audience would miss the connection between the little word *AT* in **Genesis 1** and his opening phrase. So he explains:

> This one (ie the Word) was in the beginning and everything was made through Him and nothing was made without Him. **John 1:2–3**

John is linking Jesus to Creation via **Psalm 33:6** where it says:

> By the *Word of YHWH* the heavens were made . . . by the Spirit of His Mouth.

In John's day, religious thinkers had already spotted that sometimes the 'Word of *YHWH*' acted in its own right. It was more than just a message, it was a two-way mediator between Creation and Creator. So in the Targums, the Aramaic versions and commentaries on the Old Testament, the Rabbis used a specific word whenever they saw 'the Word' acting as a distinct agent.

That Aramaic word is *Memra*. It was used by the Targums for the Hebrew *dabar* / דבר / 'word' in **Psalm 33:6** above, so making the *'Word of YHWH'* an active agent in Creation.

In John's day the Targums were passed on orally and, although we have fragments dating back to the first century, full written versions date from around the fifth century AD.

The Greek / Septuagint version of this verse uses the Greek word *Logos* / λόγος, the same word used in **John 1:1**. We get the word 'logic' from *Logos*.

 In Greek philosophy, the *Logos* was the living wisdom that stood behind Creation. **Psalm 33** describes the *'Word of YHWH'* as the *'Spirit of His (God's) Mouth'* and so the Jewish philosopher Philo, living in Egypt contemporarily but independently of John, drew a connection between the *Memra* of the Targums and the Stoic philosophers' use of *Logos*.

Philo and John also saw the connection between the active Word / *Memra* / *Logos* with the personified 'Wisdom of God' found in **Proverbs**. Philo called this 'Wisdom', 'the first-born Son of God'. 'Wisdom' is eternally anointed and alongside God in Creation; pre-existing with Him, in the beginning and day-by-day.

 The Lord possessed me *in the beginning (b-rashyth)* of His ways. Before He made things, from then, from everlasting, I was anointed *in the beginning* before the earth existed.
Proverbs 8:22–23

Most English translations lose the reference to the word 'anointed'. Following the Septuagint they translate *nawsak* / נסך (#H5258) as 'established', but *nawsak* in its passive form, as here, is someone who has been anointed.

'Wisdom' goes on to make **six** statements about acting with *YHWH* in Creation, paralleling the **six** days of **Genesis 1**:

> When . . . (1) He established the heavens . . . (2) drew a circle around the deep . . . (3) made the sky . . . (4) made the springs of the deep . . . (5) set boundaries for the sea . . . (6) marked out the foundations of the earth. Then I was the master builder by His side. I was a delight day-by-day, always happy before Him, happy in the world His Earth and my delight was with the children of men. **Proverbs 8:27–31**

It is interesting to note that 'Wisdom' is a master builder alongside God in Creation, and in life Jesus was a builder by profession too. The word our Bibles translate as 'carpenter', see **Mark 6:3**, is *tekton* which is actually the Greek word for a 'builder' (see also section *The Formation of Mankind*, p54).

Like 'Wisdom', *AT* was active with Multi-God on six occasions in **Genesis 1:1–2:3**. *AT* is there on day seven, but on day three *Elohim* acts without the word *AT*. Perhaps there is a reason why *AT* [First-and-last, binding-covenant, wounded-God, the-biggest-sacrifice-on-a-cross] is not explicitly involved on the third day, the day when God brings solid ground out of the chaotic water and new life appears, but we will consider that when we look at Noah.

'Wisdom' and the 'Word of *YHWH*' are there in **Genesis 1:1** as the little word *AT*. *AT* appears just over 200 times in the Creation and Primeval History sections of Genesis. We will not list them all, but you may want to research them for yourself with an interlinear Bible.

Now, before we get into the main text of Genesis, there is one more thing to note about the connection between the Word, Wisdom, $\forall +$ / AΩ / A to Z, and Jesus.

Ⓟ Jesus and Everything that can be Said

Over 400 years before Jesus came, the Greeks had adopted a habit from the Jewish Rabbis of enumerating words to arrive at numbers. The Jews had first caught the habit from the Assyrians during their period in exile there, and the Greeks who eventually conquered the Babylonian empire, picked up the habit then. The Greeks kept their system simple, they just added up the value of the letters in a word. Over time, the Rabbis went on to develop much more complex and varied ways of producing a number from a word which became the basis of Jewish Kabbalah.

But, in its early days, enumerating words was simply a tool of the scribes that aided accurate scripture transmission. We looked briefly at Jewish Gematria in *Volume 1: Jesus in the Old Testament*.

Now if you enumerate the Greek version of Jesus' name (as we have it in the New Testament), you get the number '888', a trinity of eights. Early Christians spotted this very quickly, because finding hidden connections in the enumerated sums of people's names was like doing the daily crossword for the ancient world's thinkers, whether philosophers or mystics, and John seems to have a touch of both of these characters about him. So, in Revelation we find John has encoded the name 'Nero Caesar' as the number '666' and linked it to the demonic beast, although to hide the obvious reference to the reigning emperor, John first translated Nero's name into Hebrew before enumerating it.

> He who has understanding, let him calculate the number of the beast, for it is the number of a man. His number is six hundred sixty-six.
> **Revelation 13:18**

We know this because later manuscripts of Revelation, written well after Nero was history, replace the number '666' with '616' which is the name and title 'Nero Caesar' enumerated straight from the Greek so there was no longer the need to be discreet.

So I'm sure John was aware as he wrote down the name 'Jesus' in Greek that it enumerated to '888'.

'Nero Caesar' translated into Hebrew as *NronQsr* / קשר נרונ gave a trinity of sixes, whereas 'Jesus' translated from Hebrew into the Greek *Iesous* / Ιησοῦς gave a trinity of eights:

> Nero Caesar / נרונ קשר :
> ר/200 + ש/60 + ק/100 + נ/50 + ו/6 + ר/200 +
> נ/50 = 666

> Jesus / Ιησοῦς:
> Ι / 10+η / 8+σ / 200+o / 70+ῦ / 400+ς / 200 =
> 888

What is more, the number '888' had special significance in Greek enumeration. It was the number associated with the whole Greek alphabet, because the Greek numbering system broke the 24 letters of the Greek alphabet into three groups of 8 letters. The first group of 8 letters enumerated digits, the second group the tens and the third group of eight the hundreds.

Three '8's covered the whole alphabet. John doesn't represent Jesus by the number '888', but Jesus does call Himself the 'Alpha-α and Omega-ω', the 'A to Z', 'the full alphabet' in John's Revelation.

We are seeing a deeply theological picture emerge

here. God is unknowable unless He reveals Himself and even then, there will be aspects of who He is that are unfathomable to us. Jesus wasn't just a man with a message, He was the embodiment of all that the inscrutable Creator God could or would reveal about Himself to Creation.

 If we know the unknowable parts of God as 'Father' it is because we know them through the knowable 'Son'. Everything that can be said into our world about God is communicated to us by the living Word; written in all the letters of a full life by Jesus the anointed, eternally emergent first-born child of the Father.

So it shouldn't be a surprise to find that from the beginning, Genesis provides us with a message and ideas that encompass the entire Gospel, the whole Bible and even the whole of history. There is a form of typology in the rhythms and events of the first half of Genesis that are paralleled, completed and fulfilled by the rest of Scripture. You can see them particularly clearly in the Book of Revelation.

 This is a good point to transfer some notes into your Bible

Ⓑ Revelation AT Last

John's apocalypse starts with the words: 'The Revelation of Jesus Christ', **Revelation 1:1a**. The book shows us Jesus before it tells us anything about the end times. One of the ways it does this is by developing and fulfilling the images and themes first found in **Genesis 1–11**.

Ideas, events and symbols that are recapitulated by / in Jesus are part of typological revelation.

The table below summarises the large number of typological connections between the Creation and primeval history of **Genesis**, and the new Creation and culmination of history in Revelation.

The first part of **Genesis** forms one of a pair of bookends with the book of Revelation. Together they encase all the other books of the Bible in a symbolic whole, a start and a finish, the Alpha-α and the Omega-ω, the Aleph-א and the Tav-ת.

Where there is a seed in **Genesis** (see **3:15**), there is fruit in **Revelation** (see **22:2**). The rest of the Bible is full of the shoots, leaves, buds and blossom of Genesis' typology as themes and ideas develop through its pages.

Connections between Genesis and Revelation

א / ע / In the Beginning . . . At the End / ‏ + ‏ / ת

Genesis 1:1 – Heaven and Earth created / formed.
Revelation 21 – New Heaven and New Earth are formed.

Genesis 1:1–2:3 – History starts with seven days of divine fiat. The word goes out and the world is formed and filled.
Revelation 5:5, 8:2,6, 10:4 – History comes to an end with seven seals, trumpet blasts and peals of thunders go out.

Genesis 1:1-2:23 – The phrase 'It was good' used seven times.
Revelation 12:12,18:10,16,19 – The word 'woe' used seven times.

Genesis 1:2, 6, 9 – Creation includes a process of dividing and bounding the waters.
Revelation 21:1 – The Sea has gone in the New Earth.

Genesis 1:21 – God makes great creatures in the Sea.
Revelation 13:2 – A beast that comes up out of the Sea.

Genesis 1:24 – Sun and moon are appointed for signs and seasons.
Revelation 21:23 – Sun and moon are no longer needed.

Genesis 2:10 – A River flowed out of Eden.
Revelation 13:2 – A River flows from the throne of God and the Lamb.

Genesis 2:12 – There is a garden containing gold, precious stones and fresh water pearls (see Moffat Bible).
Revelation 21:18–21 – There is a garden city made of gold, precious stones and pearls.

Genesis 2:22 – Adam receives a bride made from his own body after falling asleep.
Revelation 19:7 – Jesus receives a Bride made of His own body after death and resurrection.

Genesis 3:8 – Man hides from the face of God.
Revelation 22:4 – Man has permanent access to the face of God.

Genesis 3:14 – The snake in the garden is cursed to wriggle in the dirt.
Revelation 12:3, 9, 20:2 – A dragon, the serpent of old, is thrown down onto earth.

Genesis 3:14–19 – A curse is released. Death spreads to all.
Revelation 20:14, 22:3 – Death is destroyed and the curse is gone.

Genesis 3:24 – The Tree of Life is restricted.
Revelation 22:2 – The Tree of Life is multiplied.

Genesis 4:4 – The first animal sacrifice is acknowledged by God.
Revelation 5:12 – Thousand upon thousands acknowledge the value of the last sacrifice, the Lamb slain.

Genesis 9:13–16 – The rainbow is given as a sign of an everlasting Covenant of grace.
Revelation 4:3 – The rainbow surrounds. the throne of judgement.

Genesis 10:8–9 – We meet, Nimrod, the first world leader opposed to '*YHWH*'.
Revelation 19:19 – The beast leads the kings of the earth against Jesus.

Genesis 11:4 – Men build a city with a tower to reach Heaven from Earth.
Revelation 21:10 – The New Jerusalem descends to Earth from Heaven to unite God and Mankind.

The Gospel in Creation

Genesis gives us an alphabet and the start of a vocabulary of symbols that relate to Jesus and the rest of the Bible. But we don't have to wait for Revelation to find the fruit of these ideas, there are strong connections between **Genesis** and the Gospels too. In fact the very first chapter of **Genesis** gives us structures and phrases that get picked up by the Evangelists.

John starts his Gospel with the same phrase as **Genesis**, and Mark and Luke both use the word 'beginning' in their opening sentences too: '*The beginning* of the Gospel of Jesus Christ . . . ', **Mark 1:1**; '. . . those who from *the beginning* were eyewitnesses . . .' **Luke 1:2**.

So two Gospels (**Mark** and **John**) start with the same word as **Genesis 1. Note:** the first English word of the Bible, 'in', is actually a part of the Hebrew word for 'beginning' indicated by the prefix letter בּ, it is not a separate word. The third Gospel includes that word in its opening statement (**Luke**); and the fourth (**Matthew**) starts with the phrase 'The Book of Genesis . . . '

One Gospel might be a co-incidence, two would be interesting but the fact that all four Gospels reference **Genesis** in their opening statements, should flag a connection between Creation and the Gospel.

At a basic level, the Early Church Fathers saw a parallel between the days of Creation and the process of personal salvation or transformation.

Starting with the coming of light, the formless and empty Creation is formed and filled until the image of God is seen on Earth. And so it is in us: Father takes the initiative to bring each person into light – He forms us then He fills us.

Paul describes the process:

> God who said, 'Light shall shine out of darkness' is the one who has shone in our hearts, the brightness of the knowledge of the glory of God in the face of Jesus Christ. **2 Corinthians 4:6**

This is fun to see, but is more of a preacher's sermon outline than the deep things of God. There is more going on in the first chapter of Genesis than just this.

An obvious pattern in the Creation account is the use of seven days to complete Creation. Both John and Mark reflect the seven-fold pattern of Creation in the structure of their Gospels; John is probably done self-consciously, whereas Mark's pattern emerges as though subconsciously Spirit-woven into his text.

Seven Full Days in Mark

Mark's Gospel is divided into seven completed literary days: seven times, a day finishes and a new one starts. The events that fill up the text between these transitions actually take place over multiple days; the days are literary not literal. For instance day one concludes: 'And when evening had come, after the sun had set . . . ', **Mark 2:32**; and day two starts three verses later, 'in the early morning, while it was still dark . . . ', **Mark 2:35**. As in **Genesis 1**, 'An evening and a morning' mark the end of one day and the start of the next.

In **Genesis**, the seventh day is left hanging; it has a start but no completion. God rests but doesn't rise again and the day is left unfinished.

In Mark's Gospel, Jesus' seventh day starts on Good Friday, 'and early in the morning the chief priests with the elders and scribes . . . led Him away', **Mark 15:1**. Jesus is put to death and rests in the grave right through the Saturday. Unlike **Genesis**, the Sabbath ends, 'and when the Sabbath was over . . . ' and a new week starts on the Sunday, 'and early on the first day of the week . . . ', **Mark 16:1–2**.

In Mark's Gospel it is the eighth day, a day of new beginnings, the start of God's new Creation that is left unfinished.

Jesus' life reflects Creation Week in Mark's Gospel

Day 1 The first day starts in the 'Beginning', like **Genesis** (**Mark 1:1**) and ends 'When evening had come, when the sun had set' (**1:32**)

Day 2 'And in the early morning . . . He arose' (**1:35**) . . . 'When evening had come, He said to them, "Let's go over to the other side"' (**4:35**)

Day 3 'And when they had come to the other side' (**5:1**) . . . 'And when it was evening and the boat was in the middle of the sea' (**6:47**)

Day 4 'And when they had crossed over, they came to land' (**6:53**) . . . 'He departed, since it was already late' (**11:11**)

Day 5 'And on the next day . . .' (**11:12**) . . . 'And when evening came they would go out of the city' (**11:19**)

Day 6 'And as they were passing by in the morning' (**11:20**) . . . 'And when it was evening He came with the twelve . . .' (**14:17**)

Day 7 'And early in the morning . . .' (**15:1**) . . . Jesus enters his Sabbath / 'ceasing'. Then: 'and when the Sabbath was over . . .' (**16:1**)

Day 8 'And very early on the first day of the week' (**16:2**) . . . This new day never ends

Mark presents Jesus' life as a prophetic reworking of the Creation Week, complete with a day of rest. But Mark concludes it with a new day to mark a new age.

 John's Light Shines in the Darkness

The connection between John's Gospel and the first chapter of **Genesis** seems far more consciously deliberate than it does in Mark's. It is deeper too.

John saw Jesus as the Logic of God and as the Word, active in the creative miracles of each day of Creation. Seven times God speaks and then something miraculous happens, the word that God speaks becomes incarnate in Creation. This process of incarnation is symbolised in **Genesis** as the coming of light, not just on the first day but on every other day too.

You see, the phrase 'an evening and a morning' that found its way symbolically into Mark's Gospel on seven occasions, is a little subtler than it looks. Because to the Hebrew mind, the evening was not the end of a day, it was the start of a day. The Hebrew word *ereb* / ערב (#H6153), translated 'evening' means simply 'dark'. So an evening was the dark start of a day. Taking the translation a bit deeper we find that ערב is also a root word *arab* (#H6148) which is used for things that are mixed or mingled, such as woven cloth, or a swarm of insects. In this mixed sense the root can even be a 'pledge', 'mortgage' or 'surety', because these are all part payments. To be consistent we should understand *ereb* as 'twilight' or even 'starlight', ie dark but with some light in it.

Now, the Hebrew word for 'morning' in this passage contains the idea of light *breaking out* or *breaking through*. It is similar in idea to the English 'daybreak'. So you get a better feel of the phrase 'an evening and a morning' if you read it as:

> *A start of twinkling darkness and a breaking of daylight.*

There is a process here. Creation is the coming of light as each day moves from twilight, through dawn, to mid-day sun. The incomprehensible God speaks and His Word then becomes real in Creation. Obscurely and faintly at first, perhaps evening getting darker for a while until full daylight comes. So the word goes out '. . . *let the seas teem with life* . . .' and becomes tangible '. . . *and it was so'*, **Genesis 1:20a**.

The word God speaks into Creation becomes a real part of it. This process is described as the coming of light because the thing the word becomes reveals the invisible God to us. Or as Paul puts it:

> What is known about God is evident . . . because God made it evident . . . for since the creation of the world His invisible attributes, His eternal

> power and divine nature have been clearly
> seen, being understood through what has been
> made . . . **Romans 1:19–20**

So every day of Creation is presented as the coming of
light into darkness. John goes on to explain:

> In Him (Jesus) was life, and the life was the light
> of men. The light shines in the darkness . . .
> **John 1:4–5a**

John saw in Jesus' life, the ultimate incarnation, and
therefore the ultimate revelation, of God's word and
wisdom. The life of Jesus was the ultimate revelation.
In Creation we see God in the twilight but Jesus was the
breakthrough of day, His 'life was the light of men'.

Every time Jesus spoke about His life, and each time He
performed a miracle there was something happening that
paralleled the process of Creation where God spoke and
life took a step forward.

So John structured the first half of his Gospel around
seven *words* about life interwoven with seven miraculous
works which John calls *signs*. Jesus preaches about life,
then life comes by way of a miracle, 'light shines in the
darkness', **John 1:5**.

The tables on pages 32 and 33 list first the seven words or
sermons and then the seven signs or miracles.

This is a good point to transfer some notes into your Bible

The Number 7 - ז - ☰

Seven sermons and seven miracles in John. Seven literary days in **Mark**. Jesus' kingly genealogy in **Matthew** is arranged around the number seven: 42 (6 × 7) ancestors of Jesus are presented in three groups of 14 (2 × 7). Jesus' 'natural' genealogy (through Mary) makes Jesus the 77th generation from Adam.

There is some argument about the number of names in Luke's list, *Admin* (**Luke 3:33**) doesn't appear in all manuscripts. I have based my statement on the list given by the NASB and related translations.

The significance of the number '7' goes back to the Creation narrative, **Genesis 1:1–2:3**; it is explicit and implicit in the text. In addition to being structured around seven days:

- The word 'God' appears thirty-five (5 × 7) times

- The word 'Earth' appears twenty-one (3 × 7) times

- The phrase 'it was so' seven times

- The phrase 'it was good' seven times

- The first verse of **Genesis** is made of seven words and twenty-eight (4×7) letters

- The second verse has fourteen (2×7) words

- The seventh day is described in thirty-five (5×7) words and contains three seven-word sub-clauses

- The word *AT*, the hidden reference to Jesus, appears fourteen times (2×7) establishing it as a divine word in the Creation narrative

Seven-fold imagery is a thread that runs from the beginning throughout the whole Bible. There are seven saviours in the book of **Judges**, seven priests with seven trumpets led the procession around Jericho for seven days in the book of **Joshua**, the menorah had seven lights on it etc. But the book of **Revelation** uses the number seven symbolically more than any other book of the Bible, highlighting again how it concludes what **Genesis** starts. There are seven churches, seven angels, seven seals and seven trumpet blasts, seven thunders, seven bowls of wrath, seven woes, the name 'Jesus' appears seven times as does the name and title 'Jesus Christ'.

So what is so special about the number seven and how does it relate to Jesus who, as we have seen, enumerates to a trinity of '8's?

The Full Promise

The Hebrew word for '7' is *sheba* (#H7651), spelt with three Hebrew letters (from right to left), שבע. When **Genesis** was written Hebrew didn't include vowel markers so these same three letters also represent other words with different Strong's numbers. We would now distinguish שבע as: *shaba* (#H7650) which is a 'formal promise', an 'oath' or a 'covenant'; and *saba* (#H7649) which means to 'make full' or as an adjective, to be 'full'. So linguistically the number seven implied the making of a full promise or a promise that was full.

But notice that fully promising something is different from fulfilling a promise. Jesus said that the Law, by which He meant at least everything written by Moses and possibly the entire Old Testament, was full or complete but that He still needed to fulfil it, **Matthew 5:17–18**.

Things that come in sevens are exemplars communicating a promise that is looking for an ultimate and divine fulfillment:

– Seven days of Creation demand a 'day of the Lord', a resurrection day

– Seven sprinklings of blood for the forgiveness of sins in Leviticus demand a final pouring out of blood for the many, **Mark 14:24**

The 7 Words in John's Gospel

Word/Sermon	Passage	Life References
New Birth/Eternal Life	John 3:1–21	John 3:15–16
Water of Life	John 4:1–38	John 4:14
Giver of Life	John 5:19–47	John 5:21, 26, 40
Bread of Life	John 6:32–51	John 6:33,35,40, 47–48, 51
River of Living Water	John 7:37–38	John 7:38
Light of Life *(Note the 'I am' verses:*	John 8:12–59 *John 8:24, 28, 58)*	John 8:12
Abundant Life *(Note the 'I am' verses:*	John 10:7–18 *John 10:7–9, 11, 14)*	John 3:15–16

The 7 Signs in John's Gospel

Sign / Miracle	Passage	Sign References
Water into wine	John 2:1–11	John 2:11
Healing the Official's son from a distance	John 4:46–54	John 4:54
Bethesda healing on the Sabbath	John 5:1–6:2	John 6:2
Feeding 5000	John 6:3–14	John 6:14
Walking on water	John 6:16–22	John 6:26
Healing the man born blind	John 9:1–38	John 9:16
Raising Lazarus	John 11:1–45	John 11:47, 12:18

- Seven lamps on the menorah promise the 'light of the world'

- Seven national saviours in Judges point to a world saviour

Jesus, the '888', raised on Mark's eighth day (the first day of a new week) is the divine fulfillment of the promise implicit in the things that came in sevens. As Paul puts it, Jesus provides the *'Yes'* and *'Amen'* of every promise of God, **2 Corinthians 1:20**.

While not as ubiquitous as the number seven, eight is used in the Old Testament to point to a new start, a breaking in to a cycle of sevens with the substance of the promise hoped for:

- Eight people came through the flood and received the new covenant of the rainbow, **Genesis 7:13, 9:9**

- Boys were circumcised on the eighth day; having lived seven days under the law the flesh was prophetically cut off and thrown away

- Aaron and the priests start acting as priests on the eighth day after a week of cleansing, **Leviticus 8:31–9:1**

- The eighth-day pattern is repeated by Hezekiah to cleanse and rededicate the Temple, **2 Chronicles 29:17**

It is interesting to note that David is described as the

seventh son of Jesse, **1 Chronicles 2:15**, but he is the eighth son to be presented to Samuel, **1 Samuel 16:10**.

We will explore why and how this might be in *Volume 7: Jesus in the United Nation,* but here it is worth noting that in the natural, as the seventh born son, David became the repository of *promises* about the future Messiah. But prophetically, as the eighth son in rank, he is anointed as a prototype of the Messiah to come. Perhaps because the number eight was associated with grace.

In the alphabet table at the back of *Volume 1: Jesus in the Old Testament* we noted the number eight was written with the letter Heth-ח which in its pictographic development (𐤇 ⊞ ⱈ ⱨ ח) represented a **doorway** or a **way-through** a **wall** or **fence**.

Heth-ח is one of just two letters in the Hebrew word for grace / חן, the other being the sofit form of the letter Nun-ן (pictogram ↘). Nun-ן could mean seed or offspring. From the perspective of Hebrew wordplay, *grace* is *eight-offspring*, the son all those sevens have been promising.

There is a bit more to say on Jesus as the offspring who is the way-through of grace, but we will leave it until we look at the life of Noah.

Here, I want to explore how the idea of a natural seven anticipating a spiritual eight works with the seven days of Creation.

 The 7ᵗʰ Day as a Predictive Prophecy

The Bible uses the days of Creation in **Genesis** both as historic (ie they have already happened), but also as prophetic (ie they are going to happen, or they are continually happening). When asked about keeping the Sabbath, Jesus declares that He works because the Father continues to work, **John 5:17**, implying He is still in day six, God hasn't yet rested at one level. But on Good Friday, Jesus will cry out, 'It is finished', **John 19:30**, echoing the statement of **Genesis 2:2**:

> *By the seventh day* God had *finished* His work . . .
> and He *rested on the seventh day*.

The reading above is based on the Masoretic Hebrew of the Old Testament. The older Greek text, the Septuagint clarifies the meaning of 'By the seventh day', it says explicitly:

> *On the sixth day God finished His work . . . and*
> *He rested on the seventh day.*

Good Friday, the day Jesus finished His work was the sixth day of the Jewish week. Then on the seventh day, Saturday, Jesus rested in the grave. Jesus rose again on a Sunday, the first or eighth day depending on how you look at it. As with the first Sunday, the day of Creation, there was, quite literally, a coming of light, **Matthew 28:3**.

It is interesting to note that the sixth and seventh days of Creation are described differently from the previous five days, perhaps because of their prophetic significance. They are '*the* sixth day' and '*the* seventh day', whereas days two to five are: '*a* second/third/fourth/fifth day'. Day one of Creation is unique in that it is 'Day One' not '*a / the* first day', it was a Sunday, which with Jesus' resurrection became the most seminal day in history.

The idea of Jesus as the fulfillment of the promises of God continues in the next section of **Genesis**, the chapters that cover mankind's primeval history. But before we go there, I want to highlight one last thing about Jesus in the very beginning.

Ⓟ The Expected Seed Grows Up

Jesus grew up speaking Aramaic in the home and market place, but Hebrew in the classroom and synagogue. The two languages were very close as Aramaic had developed as a patois form of Hebrew during Israel's years in diaspora. Evidence from the Dead Sea Scrolls indicates that Judean and Galilean Aramaic was very close to Hebrew, even written using the same alphabet, but there were differences.

One of the changes most obvious to a reader of the Bible is the change of the word for a son, from *ben* / בנ in classical Hebrew, (*Ben-jamin*: Son-of the right hand) to *bar* / בר in the New Testament (*Bar-tholomew*: Son-of-Talmai, or *Bar-nabas*: Son-of-encouragement).

In *Volume 1: Jesus in the Old Testament* we saw that very often the meaning of a simple Hebrew root word was captured by the meanings and pictures of the letters used to write it. And it is interesting to note the difference in symbolic meaning between *ben* / בנ and *bar* / בר.

Ben as we saw was made up of a Beth-ב, which meant 'house' or 'household' and was originally depicted as the floorplan of a tent or home, ⊓, then followed by a Nun-נ, which meant 'offspring' and was depicted as a germinating seed, ↘.

So a 'son' / *ben* was the expected seed-of-the-household. Eve is told to expect a 'seed', **Genesis 3:15**, but neither Cain nor Abel are called 'son' / *ben*. Seth is the first of Eve's children to be given the title, **Genesis 4:25**, and it is through Seth that the expected seed, Jesus, finally comes.

By the time of the New Testament, 'son' is now *bar*, spelt still with a Beth- ב meaning 'household', but now followed by a Resh-ר which meant 'head' as in 'most important'. Its pictogram was a head, ℘. The symbolic meaning of 'son' has moved from the expected child (*ben*) to the full-grown heir (*bar*), the new *head-of-the-household*.

The New Testament calls Jesus the 'head' of both the church and 'all things', **Colossians 1:18**.

There is something very quirkily satisfying in seeing the shift in the symbolic meaning of the word 'son' between the Old and New Testaments.

 Now, the word *bar* / בר does appear in the Old Testament. It is used several times in **Ezekiel** and **Daniel** which were both written in Assyria at the time when Hebrew was becoming Aramaic. But more interestingly it is used twice in much older Hebrew; once by David in **Psalm 2**, where it is a title for the Messiah, and again in **Proverbs 31**, where it is used of a king called Lemuel. *Lemuel* means 'Belonging to God' and Jewish tradition tell us that Lemuel is Solomon who is himself a type of Christ.

Strong's concordance notes that this early use of the word *bar* (#H1248) seems to reflect 'Son' as a formal title. It even suggests 'Heir' as a translation. We will explore the use of *bar* as a title in the above passages more fully in *Volume 9: Jesus in Words of Wisdom* and in *Volume 10: Jesus in Worship and Wonder,* but I wanted to flag this title here, because in one sense *bar*, Son, as a title, is the first word read in the whole of the Bible.

ⓟ The Appointed Son

As a child, Jesus would be most familiar speaking Aramaic, but He would have heard Hebrew spoken in the synagogues since He was born. Then, like all Jewish boys, He would have been taught to read the Hebrew Scriptures by His local Rabbis and Scribes.

In learning to read, Jesus would have been introduced to the first word of the opening sentence of **Genesis**, 'In the beginning', *b-rashyth* / בראשת. In common with all children learning to read, and in particular bi-lingual children, His brain would have automatically dissected בראשית in every way possible, looking for the bits He knew already, playing games with the parts to help Him remember the whole.

At some point Jesus would have noticed that *b-rashyth* could be read as two short words separated by a common prefix letter:

bar a-shyth   בר א-שית

The first word is *bar* / בר / a son or an heir (#H1248). This is the word we've just looked at and is one with which the young Jesus was more familiar than the older *ben* / בן.

The last word is *Shyth* / שית from which we get the name

Seth / שת, the name of the first person (chronologically) to be called a son / בן. *Shyth* / שית (#H7896) has a range of meanings. It typically means to 'put in place', 'to lay out / on', 'to pay attention to' or, as with the name Seth, it can mean 'to appoint'.

Prefixing *Shyth* with an Aleph-א makes the verb first person, singular and future, in other words it adds 'I will' to 'put in place', 'appoint' etc.

 So, the very first word of the Old Testament can be read as:

A Son, I will appoint

It is as though God's first statement declares a coming Son! This may not be good exegesis, in other words it is not what the author intended anyone to read, but it is there nonetheless. And I am sure that Jesus would have noticed the possibility as He grew and learned to read, starting at the beginning of the Torah scroll.

Furthermore, the statement is confirmed the first time God plainly uses the phrase 'I will appoint' or 'I will put in place'/ א-שית. In **Genesis 3:15** we read:

I will put (א-שית) enmity between . . . your seed and her seed.

This verse is a very important one (see below) and here it

is good exegesis to understand that God is appointing not just a future child, but a destiny for that child too!

God-the-Father had declared His intention to put a Son and Heir in place. This Son, the eternally emergent Word, who was active in Creation would be the seed of a woman and the seed-of-the-household (*ben*) of Adam, but He would become the new household-head (*bar*), and crush the serpent's head as it snapped at His heel.

And there is more to **Genesis** than just the beginning!

This is a good point to transfer some notes into your Bible

Part 2

Primeval History

Primeval History

The First Generations . . .

Genesis 2:4 to 4:26 is the first 'genesis' / 'generations' section in the book of beginnings (see *Appendix*). It covers: *The Generations of the Heavens and the Earth* in three acts: 'Formation', 'Fall' and 'Consequences'.

The first two acts: 'Formation' and 'Fall' create a single dramatic unit in seven mini-scenes arranged in what academics call a palistrophic structure around the moment Adam and Eve eat the fruit of the Tree of Knowledge (see table opposite).

The third act: 'Consequences' follows the aftershock of this act through seven generations into polygamy and violence.

A key development across all three acts of *The Generations of the Heavens and the Earth* is the introduction of God's name, *YHWH*.

7-fold structure of Genesis 2–3

	Actor	Events	Genesis
1	God	Makes man from the dust and puts him in a garden with the Tree of Life.	2:5–17
2	God	Creates a human partnership over the animals.	2:18–25
3	Devil and Mankind	Talk about consequences of eating the fruit.	3:1–5
4	Mankind	Eats the fruit.	3:6–8
5	God and Mankind	Talk about consequences of eating the fruit.	3:9–13
6	God	Declares the human partnership is broken, enmity with the snake.	3:14–21
7	God	Sends man from the garden and Tree of Life, and back to the dust he came from.	3:22–24

The Nail and the Hand

The word *YHWH* is sometimes called the tetragrammaton, which means 'the four letters'. The Jewish historian Josephus tells us that these four letters were all vowels.

Technically we think of them as consonantal vowels, that is consonants that can act as vowels like the letter 'Y' in English. Hebrew had four consonantal vowels: Aleph-א, Wav-ו, Hey-ה and Yod-י.

The *Cambridge English Dictionary* defines a vowel as: 'a speech sound produced by humans when the **breath** flows out through the mouth without being blocked . . .' It captures the way the ancient world thought about vowels – they were 'breaths'. The Hebrew word for 'breath' is *ruach* / רוח (#H7307), which also means 'spirit'.

So, the name *YHWH* is all spirit, or as Jesus tells us: 'God is Spirit', **John 4:24**. The tetragrammaton is made up of three of the four 'breaths' – it is a spirit-trinity. The fourth vowel, Aleph-א stood for God as a whole!

Being made up of just vowels made *YHWH* hard to say and hear and, over time, devout Jews stopped pronouncing these letters, although the Rabbis still noted that they would sound like restful breathing if they were pronounced: breathe in, *yah*; breathe out, *wheh*.

The idea of breath also goes with the idea of 'life' or 'being' and *YHWH* approximates to the causative third person form of the verb 'to be', *hayah* / הוא so *YHWH* could mean **'He causes to be'**. You will sometimes see *YHWH* translated as **'He exists'** or **'He lives'**.

Now when these four letters were written down in the original proto-siniatic pictographic script they would have looked something like this (right to left in Hebrew):

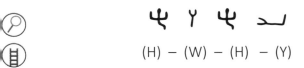

$$(H) - (W) - (H) - (Y)$$

Each pictogram had a meaning.

The first letter is the 'Y' / Yod-י / ﬞ, it shows an arm and a hand. The letter is called *Yod* which means 'hand' but it was a closed hand or a working hand to distinguish it from the letter Kaph-ק / ﬞ which was an open receiving hand (see the alphabet table in the *Appendix* of *Volume 1: Jesus in the Old Testament*).

The next letter 'H' / Hey-ה / ﬞ is shown as a person with their hands up in surprise, because the 'H' has the sound of surprise in it, *hah*. Its meaning was 'look' or 'see this'.

The last letter to consider is 'W' / Wav-ו / ﬞ, this image was a pin or tent peg or even a nail.

So *YHWH*, the tetragrammaton, the unspoken but breathed Covenant name of God implied the phrase:

> The hand, see it! The nail, see it!

Millennia later, after Jesus' resurrection, the disciple Thomas would say: 'Unless I see in His hands the print of the nails, and put my hand into His side, I will not believe.' Jesus replied: 'Put your finger here and see My hand', **John 20:25, 27.**

Kurios-er and Kurios-er

It is surprising to see Jesus' physical life and death so clearly embedded in the tetragrammaton, *YHWH,* the Covenant name of the transcendent God; a name so revered that by Jesus' day many (though not all) wouldn't even pronounce it.

The New Testament writers clearly saw the connection, because when the Greek version of the Old Testament used the word *Kurios* / 'Lord' in place of the Hebrew *YHWH*, the New Testament writers adopted *Kurios* to refer exclusively to Jesus rather than to God the Father. The only exceptions to this rule are the four times the New Testament quotes **Psalm 110:1**: 'The LORD said to my Lord . . .', a verse that highlighted Jesus as part of the Godhead anyway.

Living Promise

YHWH is a proper name. We often pronounce it 'Yahweh' though we are probably overemphasising the consonantal sounds: 'Eeaaooaa' might be more accurate. *Elohim* is more like a title, 'Multi-God', than a name.

As a name, *YHWH* is used in intimate and relational passages and is linked to the Covenant and to various promises. In particular, *YHWH* forms a compound name with eight Old Testament promises. Each promise reflects a quality of Jesus highlighted in the New Testament (see the table overleaf).

So if 'Multi-God' conveys something of the meaning of *Elohim*, perhaps 'Living-Promise' captures something of the name *YHWH*. If we allow the meaning of the original pictograms into our understanding, we might expand *YHWH* to mean:

Living-Promise [see-his-hand-see-the-nail]

As a name, *YHWH* / 'Living Promise' appears in the first verse of the first 'Generations' sub-section of Genesis, 'The Generations of the Heavens and the Earth', **Genesis 2:4**; and in its last verse, **Genesis 4:26** (**Chapter 5** starts the second sub-section of **Genesis**, see *Appendix*).

YHWH / Living-Promise Name	Seen in Jesus
YIREH: 'Living-Promise to provide', **Genesis 22:8**. Spoken by Abraham in faith for a substitute sacrifice in the foothill of Moria.	Jesus was crucified on the same foothills just outside Jerusalem as a ransom for many.
ROPHE: 'Living-Promise to Heal', **Exodus 15:26**. Given at Mara where the bitter waters are healed by a special tree.	'He healed all that were sick.' **Matthew 8:16**
NISSI: 'Living-Promise my Banner', **Exodus 17:15**. The name was associated with victory in battle.	'God who gives us the victory through Jesus Christ.' **1 Corinthians 15:57**
MCKEDDESH: 'Living-Promise your sanctifier.' **Exodus 31:13**	'We have been sanctified through the offering of the body of Jesus Christ once for all.' **Hebrews 10:10**
SHALOM: 'Living-Promise of Peace.' **Judges 6:24**	'We have peace with God through our Lord Jesus Christ.' **Romans 5:1**
ROHI: 'Living-Promise your Shepherd'. **Psalm 23:1**	'I am the Good Shepherd.' **John 10:11, 14**
TSIKENU: 'Living-Promise of your Righteousness'. **Jeremiah 23:6**	'Filled with the fruits of righteousness that come through Jesus Christ.' **Philippians 1:11**
SHAMMAH: 'Living-Promise to be There'. **Ezekiel 48:35**	'I am with you always, even to the end of the age.' Jesus in **Matthew 28:20**

In this first 'Generations' sub-section, there are 35, (5 × 7) references to *YHWH*, *YHWH Elohim* and / or *Elohim*. God is promising something. There are 40, (5 × 8) hidden references to *AT* / את / ‏𐤀𐤕. The number five was represented by the letter Hey-ה which as we have just seen meant 'look at this' or 'see it'.

It is as though we are being invited to see and be amazed, ‏𐤀, that the living-promise of multi-God (5 x 7) is fulfilled in the invisible *AT* (5 x 8), which (as we will see in section *The Promised Seed*, page 60) marks out the first reference to the *Man-God* who is implicit in God's first prophetic promise (but we'll come that).

Finally, there is a hint at God's multi-unity in *YHWH*, which can be used with plural pronouns even though it is a singular noun. This can be when it is linked to *Elohim* as in **Genesis 3:22**: 'Man has become like *one of Us*', and sometimes it is in its own right, such as in **Genesis 11:6–7**:

> And *YHWH* / Living-Promise said, 'See they are one people . . . *Let Us go* down *and We shall* confuse their language.

See also **Isaiah 6:8**.

The Formation of Mankind

When God made mankind, he/they reflected God's multi-unity. Mankind was made a 'him' and a 'them', **Genesis 1:27**. Made in God's image they were given a realm in which to exercise authority and they were commissioned to be fruitful and fill up the earth, **Genesis 1:28**. In **Genesis 2:7** God breathed His breath into mankind.

There are parallels between God and Adam, and Jesus and His disciples.

Jesus gave His disciples authority, **Luke 9:1**; He commissioned them to be fruitful, **John 15:4–8**; and to fill up the earth, **Matthew 28:19**. He also breathed His breath into them, **John 20:22**. The parallels highlight Jesus' divinity. But in Adam we also find parallels that highlight Jesus' humanity because:

> Adam . . . is a type of Him who was to come.
> **Romans 5:14**

Even the name 'Adam' pre-figures Jesus. In Hebrew *Adam* means 'red' and is related to the words for 'land' / 'earth', *adamah*. However, Adam was named before Hebrew existed as a language. In the oldest language we know anything about, Akkadian, the first man is called 'Adamu' which is a proper word.

In Akkadian, *Adam* means 'a maker', 'a producer' or 'a builder'.

Man is 'a maker' because he is made in the Maker's image. The first Adam was 'a producer' given a Garden and charged to tend it and make it fruitful. But the last Adam, Jesus, was a *tekton* / τέκτων (#G5045), which is actually the Greek word for 'a builder' – we can see it in the word Architect from *architecton* / ἀρχιτέκτων (#G753) meaning 'master builder', **1 Corinthians 3:10**. Though English Bibles follow a tradition and translate the word *tekton* as 'carpenter'.

The table on the next page highlights the parallels between Adam and Christ.

 This is a good point to transfer some notes into your Bible

Parallels between Adam and Christ

Adam (the First Man)	Jesus (the last Adam)
Was made in the image of God, **Genesis 1:26**	Is the image of the invisible God, **Colossians 1:15**
Was made a living soul, **1 Corinthians 15:45**	Was made a quickening spirit, **1 Corinthians 15:45**
From the earth, **Genesis 2:7**	From above, **John 3:31, 8:23**
Given Life, **Genesis 2:7**	Gives life, **John 5:21,25; 6:33**
Given all authority on Earth, **Genesis 1:28–30**	Given all authority in Heaven and on Earth, **Matthew 28:18**
Received a bride made from his own body, **Genesis 2:21-23**	Will receive a Bride made from His own body, **Revelation 19:7**
Was naked and unashamed, **Genesis 2:25**	Despised the shame of Cross, **Hebrews 12:2**
Pursued his own will in the Garden of Eden, **Genesis 3:6**	Submitted to the Father's will in the Garden of Gethsemane, **Luke 22:42**
Hid among the trees, **Genesis 3:8**	Was held up for all to see on the Cross, **John 19:19**
Lost access to the Tree of Life, **Genesis 3:24**	**Became the Tree of Life**
Reaped thorns as a sign of the curse, **Genesis 3:18**	Wore thorns as a sign of the curse, **Mark 15:17**

The First Christophany

Genesis 3 gives us our first concrete view of the Persons in God and of the Messiah to come. It all starts with the first physical manifestation of God described in the Bible.

The 'Word of *YHWH*' was more than just a message, more even than the logic or wisdom that stood behind Creation. The 'Word of *YHWH*' walked, talked and did things, **Genesis 15:4**; it was a Christophany, a pre-Christmas incarnation of God's Son. While the embodied 'Word of *YHWH*' doesn't explicitly appear until **Genesis 15**, it does make a sneaky appearance in **Genesis 3** as the 'Voice', marked out by the word *AT* on one side and *YHWH* on the other:

> They heard *AT* the voice of *YHWH* God walking in the garden in the breeze of the day.
> **Genesis 3:8**

'Voice' is a translation of the Hebrew *qol* / קיל (#H6963), but the Targums still translate it as *Memra* as they would have if it was *dabar* / דבר / 'word' because the 'Voice' of God was just another way of saying the same thing. Some Bibles use the phrase the 'sound of *YHWH* God' which might imply that God was crashing through the trees, but the *qol* means the sound that comes out of something, not the sound its actions make.

Genesis 3:8 is the first Christophany in the Bible; a physical, visible, touchable manifestation of God. There is also a hint of the Spirit here too. The word 'breeze' is actually *ruach* which can mean a 'wind' or the 'Spirit' (or even a vowel, see page 48). And while the phrase 'in the Spirit of the day' sounds odd we shouldn't forget that the Spirit has been brooding over every day of Creation since **Genesis 1:2**. God, who is transcendent and above Creation, is active in Creation through His incarnating, light-bringing Word and by His brooding, life-infusing Spirit.

Now as we go on we read that 'the man and his wife hid from the presence of the Lord.' The word 'presence' is actually a plural noun *panim* / פנים (#H6440) used as if it was singular, like *Elohim*. The King James version of the Bible normally translates the word as 'before', as in standing before, hence 'in the presence of'. But the King James also translates it as 'face', and as 'person', though as a plural noun these should be 'faces' or 'persons'. In *YHWH*'s presence you can't help but see the Trinity.

Genesis 3:8 explicitly connects the incarnate Voice of God to *AT* and to *YHWH*. It is the first verse to add depth to the idea of God's multiplicity, an idea hinted at from the first verse of the Bible, see **Genesis 1:1**, but also **1:26–27** and **3:22**.

We can see the Trinity in **Genesis 3:8**. Expanding the verse, we might write:

They heard *AT* [first-and-last], the [incarnate] Voice of Living-Promise Multi-God, walking in the Spirit of the Day. And the man and his wife hid themselves from the persons (faces) of Living-Promise Multi-God among the trees of the garden.

It is this incarnation of God who speaks to the serpent, to Adam and to Eve and speaks the foundational promise that becomes the Gospel. Theologians call **Genesis 3:15** the 'Proto-Evangelium' or the 'Proto-Gospel'.

The Proto-Gospel

I will put enmity between you and the woman and between your seed and her seed. He will crush your head and you will crush His heel. **Genesis 3:15**

Paul refers to this verse in **Galatians 4:4**:

When the fullness of the time came, God sent out his Son, born to a woman, born under the Law.

Genesis is the first book of the Law, so the Son '*born under the Law*' is a way of referring to the Son predicted by the Torah, a son who was the seed of a woman rather than the seed of a man. The virgin birth is anticipated here in **Genesis 3**. This seed of a woman would crush the serpent's head even as it bit at the heel that bore down on it.

The imagery of the heel crushing the head is picked up in **Psalm 68:19–23** which starts by declaring:

> Bless the Living-Promise (*YHWH*) who daily bears our burden, the Multi-God (*Elohim*) who is our **Jesus** (Salvation) . . . **And God will strike through the head of His enemies**.

Psalm 68 actually uses Jesus' name and links it to the fulfilment of the Proto-Evangelium. Eve, like so many of us, is impatient for the promise of God!

ⓟ The Promised Seed

It seems that Eve hoped this snake-crushing son would be Cain. When she becomes pregnant and gives birth she declares in our English Bibles something like: 'I have gotten that Man with *YHWH*' or 'I have gotten that man with *YHWH*'s help', **Genesis 4:1**.

Eve refers to her son as a 'man' not as a 'child'; she is seeing his destiny, not his new-born condition. And the word 'with' translates *AT*, one of the rare times it is reflected by our English Bibles.

AT has already appeared twice in the text of **Genesis 4:1**. Once it marks out the name 'Eve' and once it marks the name 'Cain'. In both of these cases *AT* plays its usual grammatical role, marking Eve and Cain as the definite objects in the sentence.

However, if *AT* played the same role before *YHWH* it would make *YHWH* an object of the verb 'gotten' / 'acquired'. So translators add a word like 'with', 'from' or 'that' between 'man' and '*YHWH*' which is legitimate (Strong's concordance marks this '*AT*' with a different number, #H254, rather than #H253 to reflect this difference in use). However, they sometimes add an extra word such as 'help' to the sentence to make God a secondary agent in the birth rather than a direct part of it, which perhaps misses the point. We could translate **Genesis 4:1** something like:

> And (AT)Eve conceived and gave birth to (AT)Cain, and said, 'I have gotten that man-*AT* / with-Living-Promise (*YHWH*).'

Eve saw her promised seed as in some way divine, entangled with *YHWH*. She was correct in seeing a divine aspect in her promised seed, but she was wrong in assuming that that-Man-ת×-with-*YHWH* would be her first child, Cain.

In the end Jesus came though Seth, Eve's third son, who only gets born after Cain murders his brother Abel and becomes the first sinner saved under the sign of the

Cross. But before we get to that let's think about Abel.

Abel's story starts before he or his brother Cain were even born.

The Blood of Abel

Having explained to Adam and Eve the consequences of their sin, God gives humanity a hint of how He is going to deal with it by clothing them in animal skins.

Adam's and Eve's deaths have been delayed, but it has cost the life of something else to cover their shame!

Now it is not statistically significant, but it is interesting to note nonetheless, that the diminutive version of Jesus' name, ישע (see *Volume 1: Jesus in the Old Testament*), appears spread out every seventh letter in **Genesis 3:21– 22**. We find it in the words for 'skin' / עור, 'he-clothed' / וילבשם and *YHWH* / יהוה.

עור	וילבשם	ויאמר	יהוה
/ Skin	And-he-/ clothed-them	And-he-said-to-them	'YHWH' /

Jesus' name is reversed in the Hebrew text, but at the time that **Genesis** was first written down writing didn't have a totally fixed direction.

Here at the foundation of human history, *YHWH* had Himself provided a model sacrifice to cover sin:

> From the foundation of the world . . . a Lamb who has been slain. **Revelation 13:8**

YHWH had even expressed the name *Ysha* / Jesus to be discovered by faith and hindsight, hidden in the words that described the sin covering quality of the first sacrifice in the Bible. But it is Abel who picks up the subtle imagery and makes it more concrete.

Hebrews 12:24 makes a wonderfully ambiguous statement about Abel as a *type* of Christ:

> To Jesus, the mediator of a new covenant, and to the blood of sprinkling that speaks better than that of Abel.

The writer doesn't clarify whether he is referring to the blood offered up by Abel or Abel's own blood spilled by his brother's jealousy.

Let's start with Abel's offering. His action is seen as an act of faith:

> By faith Abel offered God a more excellent sacrifice than Cain, by which he obtained a testimony that he was righteous, God affirming his gifts. **Hebrews 11:4**

Faith is always a response to God's initiative, 'Faith comes by hearing . . .', **Romans 10:17**; and is completed by our response, 'as a result of the actions, faith was completed', **James 2:22**.

Although Abel wasn't born at the time of *YHWH*'s first sacrifice, he must have heard from his parents that a sacrifice was involved in covering their vulnerability and deferring the death that came via sin. So, by faith, Abel's offering from his livestock was a response of faith to a work of God that he had been told about. In this, Abel's faith was just like ours. Abel's act acknowledged *YHWH*'s message, Abel like Adam now lived by the death of another life. And *YHWH* affirmed Abel's faith!

Cain takes this affirmation as favouritism on God's part. With hind-sight we can see *YHWH* is establishing a testimony in Abel's blood offering that prepares our understanding for Jesus and the work of the Cross. But Cain's affront leads to Abel's death, which adds to Abel's testimony.

Abel is now a type of Jesus too, as: a good shepherd, a righteous and innocent man who died because of someone else's sin, **Matthew 23:35**.

The Mark of Cain

God confronts Cain with the murder of his brother, but in His mercy God offers to put a 'sign' or 'mark' on Cain, to preserve his life. This mark is an extention of the grammatical marker word *AT / 𐤕𐤀* which spoke pictographically of a sacrifice, a bull on crossed sticks; a burnt offering to the Old Testament mind, but Calvary in the New Testament.

The Hebrew word used for the 'mark' is *AWT / אות* (#H225). It adds a Wav-ו between the Aleph-א and the Tav-ה of *AT*.

The original pictogram form of Wav-ו was '𐤉', a tent peg, a pin or a nail. We saw it in the name *YHWH* (section *The nail and the hand*, page 48).

'𐤕𐤉𐤀'

AWT is used 79 times in the Old Testament, normally as a directly given divine sign, though occasionally as a sign given by a prophet. This 'mark' is used of circumcision, the Sabbath, portents that come via the sun and moon, the rainbow, and it is the *'sign of the Covenant'*.

The mark of grace and salvation put on Cain was a blood sacrifice nailed to a cross.

This is a good point to transfer some notes into your Bible

The Lineage of Jesus – God to Noah

We noted in *Volume 1: Jesus in the Old Testament* that Jesus' ancestors from God through to Noah create an astounding prophetic statement that maps out Jesus' life:

Elohim	'God'
Adam	'Producer' / 'Maker' / 'Builder' (Akkadian)
Seth	'Is appointed'
Enosh	'Mortal (man)' / 'Failing'
Kenen	'Begotten' / 'Sorrowful' / 'Dwelling place'
Mahelel	'The Glory of God'
Jared	'Descends'
Enoch	'A teacher' / 'To dedicate'

Methuselah 'His death shall bring'

Lamech 'Depraved' / 'Humble'

Noah 'Rest' / 'Comfort'

Put together this reads:

> *God, a builder, is appointed as a mortal dwelling place, begotten and sorrowful. The glory of God descends to dedicate / a teacher. His death shall bring the depraved / humble rest.*

We've already noted that Jesus was a builder in life.

 # Enoch as a Type of Christ

Enoch means 'to dedicate' or 'a teacher'. He appears in Jesus' genealogy and had an important role in ancient Jewish culture as the prototype prophet / teacher.

The Old Testament records that Noah's flood came the year after Enoch's son Methuselah died, and Methusaleh means 'His death shall bring (it)'. In the natural, Enoch had prophesied judgement and wrath, but when you see the hidden prophecy in Jesus' lineage we can see that Enoch had prophesied grace and rest as well as judgement through his son's name.

In the New Testament, Jude quotes another prophecy from Enoch:

> See, the Lord comes . . . to execute judgement and convict the ungodly . . . **Jude 14–15**

It is probably part of Enoch's vision of the coming flood, but Jude sees this prophecy as relating to Jesus' second coming. It is not unusual for prophecies to have both an immediate and an ultimate fulfillment.

Jewish folklore assigns all sorts of miracles and prophecies to Enoch. Now **Genesis** tells us that:

> Enoch walked with God and was not. **Genesis 5:24**

And **Hebrews 11:5** tells us that this verse means Enoch was translated or ascended into heaven, because of his faith. So Enoch becomes a model as a dedicated, prophetic teacher who ascends to heaven, a model filled out by Elijah and fulfilled by Jesus.

 Noah as a Type of Christ

> By faith, Noah, being warned about things not yet seen . . . prepared a ship for the saving of his house . . . and became heir of the righteousness that is by faith. **Hebrews 11:7**

Noah was the first world saviour, creating a model by which to understand Jesus. At a simple level Noah:

- *Came* through the waters (see overleaf)

- Was a 'righteous man, perfect in his generations' **Genesis 6:9b**

- 'Walked with God', **Genesis 6:9c**

- Did what the Father told him to do, **Genesis 6:22**

- Was 'a preacher of righteousness', **2 Peter 2:5**

- Saved his household from judgement, sons and brides, **Genesis 6:18**

- Was given all authority, **Genesis 9:2b**

- Received a new Covenant, **Genesis 9:5**

- Drank new wine in a new age, **Genesis 9:21**

- Removed the distinctions between clean and unclean animals, **Genesis 9:3**, see also **7:2** and **Acts 10:13–15**

- Became the judge of nations, **Genesis 9:25–26**

But there are also a couple of features of Noah's story that require a deeper look.

🅱 *A Saviour Through Water*

Noah and the Ark are specifically referenced by the New Testament as being a type of Jesus in that they came through the waters of baptism and death to save the world:

> . . . God waited patiently in the days of Noah while the Ark was being built. In it only a few people, eight in all, were saved through water, and this water symbolizes baptism that now saves you also . . . It saves you by the resurrection of Jesus Christ. **1 Peter 3:20–21**

The New Testament presents baptism as a sacrament that prophetically identifies the participant with the death and resurrection of Jesus. Jesus Himself goes through the sacrament before living out its truth.

Noah is the first Old Testament character to come through or lead through water. Others include Moses, who was drawn out of the Nile as a child before leading the Israelites through the Red Sea, and Joshua who came through the Red Sea to lead the Israelites through the Jordan into Canaan. Most famously Jonah spends half of all the verses in his book in or at sea before bringing salvation to gentile Nineveh.

The ancient world saw the sea / waters as chaotic, moving, uncertain. To be overwhelmed by waters was to be trapped in death and decay.

In the Creation narrative of **Genesis 1**, the raw stuff of creation is described as a formless and empty ocean. That chaos is then formed and filled over the six days. It is on the third day of Creation that land appears in the midst of the waters and life occurs for the first time. We noted, (in section *The Logic of God*, page 12) that on the third day of Creation God acted, but *AT* didn't, perhaps a prophetic hint towards the Father raising His Son on the third day: 'The God of our fathers raised up Jesus . . .', **Acts 5:30**.

The third day of Jesus' death was Easter Sunday, the 5th April 33 AD. But the day Jesus 'rested' in the tomb, Saturday 4th April, was anticipated by the day Noah's Ark came through the flood and rested.

 *Three Days After Passover?*

Genesis 8:4 tells us that the Ark came to rest on the 17th day of the 7th month, the month of *Abib*. In **Exodus 12:1** God re-set the religious calendar so that the old 7th month became the new 1st month, because this was the month of Israel's new beginning. Centuries later the Israelites were deported in Exile to live in Assyria, then Babylon. When they returned to their homeland the names of the

months had changed. *Abib* was now called *Nisan*.

The name *Nisan* / ניסד was borrowed from the Assyrian first month, which was called *Nisannu* and while we can't be sure, it seems that *Nisannu* meant 'sacrifice' which made it an appropriate title for the month that included Passover. Its older name, *Abib*, came from a root meaning to be 'tender', 'young' or 'green'.

According to John's Gospel, Jesus died on the day of preparation for the Passover feast, ie during the day on *Nisan* 14th. This was a Friday and Jesus rose on the Sunday, three partial days but only two full days after Passover, ie *Nisan* 16th, a whole day before the day we're interested in, *Nisan* 17th.

According to the Gospels nothing really happened on *Nisan* 17th. So, it doesn't look as though the date of the Ark's arrival on Ararat fits with the events of the first Easter.

But, in the last half century, it has become apparent that the 17th of *Abib* is not quite the same as the 17th of *Nisan*. It seems that the Jews bought other changes to their Calendar back with them from their time in Exile, it wasn't just a name change. One change in particular (though not mentioned in the Bible), does solve a number of apparent contradictions and puzzles in both the Old and New Testaments.

That change was to how a new month was observed. Assyria marked the start of their months by the arrival of a new moon, but the Egyptians used the older and easier to observe disappearance of the old moon, to mark the end of the previous month and the start of the next.

A new moon is first visible between 1 and 3 nights after the waning of the old moon. When the Israelites left Egypt, they would have been counting their months in step with the Egyptians, just as they would align their calendar with the Assyrians centuries later during the exile.

In 33 AD, there were two days difference between the start of the renamed *Nisan* and the start of its old self, *Abib*. So, the 17th of *Abib* was actually *Nisan* 15th. The date that the Ark had come to rest, was the same day of the year that Jesus rested in the grave. April 4th 33 AD was a Sabbath, a day of rest, a Saturday!

Jesus lay in the ground on the anniversary of the day that Noah's Ark had touched solid ground on the mountains of Ararat.

Now the name, *Ararat* / אררט (#H780) was not a Hebrew word, but if it was it would come from *arar* / ארר (#H779) which means 'a curse', and *yarat* / ירט (#H3399) which means 'to be contrary' or 'to turn over'. To the Hebrew ear and way of thinking, *Ararat* means, 'a curse turned over' or 'a curse reversed', which makes its date connection with Easter even more significant. Friday was the day the curse did its worst, Saturday was the day the curse was turned over, Sunday was the start of a whole new era.

The Atoning Ark

Believers have seen a type of Christ in Noah's Ark since they were first called Christians. The Ark is clearly a vessel of salvation but, as such, it is more a model of the Church, Christ's body, than of Jesus as an individual.

But the Early Church Fathers noted that the Ark was wooden like the Cross; had many rooms like the place Jesus is preparing for us; and a single door to enter by. And perhaps most interestingly, the Ark was covered inside and out with pitch / bitumen.

The Hebrew word for 'pitch' / *kaphor* / כפר (#H3724) comes from the same root *kapher* / (#H3722) as the mercy-seat on the Ark of the covenant, *kaphoreth* / כפרת (#H3727). The root can also mean 'a redemption price'. Jesus is called our *redemption*, **Hebrews 9:12**, and He is called the *mercy-seat* or *propitiation* in **Romans 3:25** (using the same Greek work, *hilasterion* / ἰλαστήριον (#G2435) used in the Septuagint to translate *kaphoreth* / כפרת).

Noah's Ark is the first example of a 'place of covering / mercy' a type, along with the mercy-seat on the Ark, of which Jesus is the anti-type, the propitiation for sin modelled by both Arks.

 # The Soothing Aroma

When Noah finally leaves the Ark, he builds the first Altar in history and offers up a burnt offering. Then we read:

> *YHWH* smelled the pleasant aroma. *YHWH* said in His heart, 'I will not again curse the ground any more for man's sake . . .' **Genesis 8:21**

The phrase 'soothing aroma' is used to describe the satisfactional effect of Noah's sacrifice. Theologians use the word satisfactional to describe the work of the Cross in terms of its effect within God. The Cross satisfies God's honour and His justice, it soothes His anger and frustration. We will explore the satisfactional dimension of the Cross more theologically in *Volume 5: Jesus in the Wilderness*, but here I just want to highlight something about the phrase itself.

 In **Genesis 8:21** 'soothing aroma' is made up of eight letters and it contains the letter Heth-ח three times. (Note: Heth-ח stands for the number 8, see the alphabet table in the Appendix of *Volume 1: Jesus in the Old Testament*).

ריח הניחח

So, the 'soothing aroma', the satisfying effect of sacrifice contains a trinity of '8's just as we saw the name *Jesus* enumerates to '888' in the New Testament, (see section *Jesus and Everything that can be Said*, page 15).

 This is a good point to transfer some notes into your Bible

 **The Name of the Healer**

Before Noah dies at the end of **Genesis 9**, he blesses one of his sons, Shem, and curses his grandson, Canaan, to serve Shem. This is the first hint in the Bible of the connection between the land of Canaan and Shem's descendants, the Israelites. Then in **Genesis 10** the nations spread out into different territories and we read the first description of Canaan, the Promised Land, **Genesis 10:19**.

At the start of **Genesis 11**, rebellious mankind says: 'Come on let's make a name for ourselves', **Genesis 11:4b**. And although the builders of Babel didn't know it, God was already making a name for Himself. He hid the details in plain sight, in the names of Shem's ancestors through to Abram, names spread through Chapters **10** and **11**.

There are ten generations between Shem and Abram. We'll start with the first five names in the list because they are reasonably straightforward to translate:

Shem	'Name' / 'Fame' / 'Renown'
Arpachsad	'Healer' / 'Releaser'
Shelah	'Sent'
Eber	'To pass through' / 'From the other side'
Peleg	'Divide' / 'Separation'

Tidying up these names we get the start of a sentence:

> *The renown of the healer-releaser sent from the other-side of the divide . . .*

The names that follow are going to tell us about the things this healer-releaser is famous for. The first three names are very straightforward to translate, the last two need a bit more comment:

Reu	'Friend' (**John 15:3**) / 'Shepherd' (**John 10:11**)
Serug	'A vine' (**John 15:4–5**)
Nahor	'A lamp' (**John 12:46**), can also be 'snoring'
Terach	'A wanderer' / 'Marked by the Spirit'
Abram	'Exalted Father' / 'Raised by the Father'

Technically *Terach* is a pagan name. You'll normally see it translated as 'wild goat' or 'wanderer', but these are just guesses. We should note that Hebrew ears would have heard the word *ruach* in the *Terach*, and *ruach* means 'spirit' or 'breath'. In Hebrew the Tav-ת could be used as a prefix to emphasise or amplify a verb. So *Terach* could be 'very spirited' or 'marked by the Spirit'.

Abram is made up of two unambiguous words, *Ab* means 'father' and *ram* means to 'lift up' or 'raise up' – hence the standard 'exalted Father'. However, there is no reason to translate the words in that order, they can equally be translated 'Father raised' or 'raised by the Father'.

Putting everything together we get:

> *The renown of the healer-releaser sent from the other-side of the divide – the friend, a shepherd, a lamp, marked by the Spirit raised by the Father.*

Jesus the Teacher

In the names of Jesus' ancestors from God to Noah we see that Jesus would move from being 'a builder' into being 'a teacher' when 'the glory of God' 'descended' on Him (see section *The Lineage of Jesus*, *God to Noah*, page 66). And in fact we read in the Gospels that after the Spirit came on Jesus at His baptism, 'He went all around Galilee teaching . . .' **Matthew 4:23**.

Like Paul, Jesus' approach to resolving complex issues was to find the first or earliest reference to something that affected the issue. He gave precedence to 'from the beginning . . .' **Matthew 19:8, Mark 10:6**.

The table on the next page highlights the verses and ideas from **Genesis 1–11** referenced by Jesus the Teacher.

Jesus' Teachings from Genesis 1–11

Jesus	Idea	Genesis
Matthew 19:4–5 Mark 10:6–8	God created them male and female . . .	1:27
	. . . the two will become one flesh	2:24
Luke 10:19	Tread on serpents	3:15
John 8:44	The devil is a murderer and a liar from the beginning	3:2–4, 24
Matthew 23:35 Luke 11:51	The blood of righteous Abel	4:8
Matthew 15:19	Evil is from the heart	6:5
Matthew 24:37–38 Luke 17:26-27	As it was in the days of Noah	6:8–7:24
Matthew 24:37	Live by the sword die by the sword	9:6
John 15:5,8,16	Be fruitful . . .	1:28
Matthew 28:19 Mark 16:15–16	. . . fill up the earth with God's image	9:1,7

Conclusion

God's original commission to mankind was to be fruitful, to fill the earth (with His image), and to exercise dominion over it, **Genesis 1:27–28**. God restated that commission to Noah when He established His New Covenant with Creation through mankind, **Genesis 9:1–17**. And Jesus' final Great Commission to His followers follows the same pattern. They are to multiply and spread God's image by making disciples, **Matthew 28:19–20a**, spreading His Covenant to all Creation and exercising authority over it, **Mark 16:15–18**.

As we allow Christ to be formed in us and we make disciples, we find ourselves aligned with the Father and Son's original vision for the world, to fill it with His image.

You can search the Scriptures for life, **John 5:39**, but be unchanged by them even though they are powerful. Scripture is supposed to lead us to Jesus. So dialogue with the Lord as you read and study, to turn facts you've found here into revelation and encounters with Him.

. . . this brings us to the end of our look at **Genesis 1–11**. We will pick up the story of Jesus in the Old Testament in the next volume:

3
Jesus in the Fathers

Patriarchs & Promises

Genesis 12 – 50

Summary

In **Genesis 1–11** we have seen Jesus revealed in many ways:

 Jesus has been prophesied as the Woman's seed who will crush the serpent's head.

 Jesus has been modelled by the first world saviour, Noah, whose labour of love and faith saves his extended family.

 We have discovered words, ideas and characters referenced by Jesus, peppered through the text. And we've found Jesus' Great Commission in words spoken first to Adam and then to Noah

 The incredible prophecy hidden in the names of Jesus' ancestors has continued to unfold.

 Eve expected divinity in her promised seed and *YHWH* Elohim proved to be multi-layered.

 The pre-incarnate Christ has walked in the Garden with Adam – God's message made flesh.

 God's name *YHWH,* all breath or Spirit has invited us to see the scars of the Cross, the nail and the hand!

Appendix

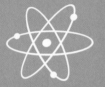

1. Traditional Structure of Genesis

The book of beginnings is actually made up of an introduction, **Genesis 1–2:3**, plus ten sections that start with the word *toledah* / 'generations' / 'genesis'.

These 10 sections are:

Toledah Section	Range
The Generations of Heaven and Earth	2:4 – 4:26
The Generations of Adam	5:1 – 6:8
The Generations of Noah	6:9 – 9:29
The Generations of Noah's sons	10:1 – 11:9
The Generations of Shem	11:10 – 11:26
The Generations of Terah (Abram's history)	11:27 – 25:11
The Generations of Ishmael	25:12 – 25:18
The Generations of Isaac	25:19 – 35:29
The Generations of Esau	36:1 – 36:43
The Generations of Jacob	37:1 – 50:26

2. The Shape of Creation

'. . . and the Earth was formless and empty . . .' – dark and chaotic

Days of formation	Days of filling

Day One: Sunday

Formed: Division and definition of Light and Darkness, **Day** and **Night**.

A Fourth Day: Wednesday

Filled: The Sun **to rule over** the **Day** and the Moon **to rule over** the **Night**.

By the end of Wednesday, two lights rule over the environment. Day and Night formed on the Sunday.

A Second Day: Monday

Formed: Division and definition of **Sea** and **Sky**.

A Fifth Day: Thursday

Filled: The **Seas** teem with fish-life, the birds fill the **Sky**.

By the end of Thursday the environment created on Monday is filled with life, but is not ruled by that life.

A Third Day: Tuesday

Formed: Drawing out **Land** from the sea and vegetation from the **Land**.

The Sixth Day: Friday

Filled: Animal life fills the land.

Then: Man is commissioned to fill the land and rule over the life that already fills **Land**, **Sea** and **Sky**.

By Friday God's work is completed, by Good Friday *'It is finished'*. Man's rule is fulfilled by the ascended Christ.

The Seventh Day: Saturday
God enters His rest

3. Genesis 1–11 in Overview

Event	Key Characters	Chapter+verse
Creation – a cosmic view	Elohim / Multi-God	1:1 – 2:3
Creation – a human view	*YHWH* / Living-Promise	2:4 – 2:25
The Fall	God, the snake, Adam, Eve	3:1 – 3:24
The success of sin – sex and violence	Cain, Abel, Lamech, Seth	4:1 – 4:26
The descendants of Adam	Adam, Seth, Enoch, Noah	5:1 – 5:32
The Flood	Noah	6:1 – 8:32
A New Covenant	Noah, Shem, Ham /Canaan, Japheth	9:1 – 9:29
The dispersal of the nations	Shem, Ham Canaan, Nimrod, Japheth, Eber	10:1– 10:32
The Tower of Babel	God	11:1 – 11:9
The descendants of Shem	Terach, Abram, Sarai	11:10 – 11:32

An invitation

Dear Reader,

On the next page you will find a list of the 14 titles in this series. The first three are complete and the rest are already in production – I have notes and rough written material on each one, but there is still a huge amount of work to turn these teaching notes into a readable resource. And the 14 Old Testament titles are only half the story – I am still shaping up the titles and format for between 10 and 12 books to cover the New Testament too. At a rate of two books a year I still have a dozen years or so of writing ahead of me!

So if you've enjoyed this book, you may not want to wait that long. And the good news is that I'm teaching this material, both live and online as well as distributing rough notes and articles all the time to an online community that helps me shape the material and get it written.

So I wanted to invite you to become a part of this community. The simplest way is to email me at *christen@jesuscentred.org* – I will email you back and explain what is happening and how you can get involved.

I won't say too much more here, because things are developing and changing all the time, but I've been making lots of friends as I produce this material and I'm always delighted to have the support of others who want to know Jesus better.

With Love and Regards,

Christen Forster
christen@jesuscentred.org

Jesus in the Old Testament Series (proposed plan)

Jesus in the Old Testament: OUT
An introduction NOW
Genesis – Malachi
978-0-9933445-1-0

Jesus in the Beginning:
Creation & Primeval History
Genesis 1 – 12   OUT
978-0-9933445-5-8 NOW

Jesus in the Fathers:
Patriarchs & Promises
Genesis 12 – 50   OUT
978-0-9933445-7-2 NOW

Jesus in the Great Escape:
Out of Egypt
Exodus
978-0-9933445-5-8

Jesus in the Wilderness:
Signs and Wanders
Leviticus – Deuteronomy
978-0-9933445-8-9

Jesus in War and Peace:
The Age of Heroes and Heroines
Joshua – Ruth

Jesus in the United Nation:
Under an anointed Prophet, Priest and King
1 &2 Samuel – 1 Kings

Jesus in Division and Defeat:
Prophetic Purpose in a Broken People
2 Kings – 1 & 2 Chronicles

Jesus in Words of Wisdom:
For Life, Love and Loss
Job – Song of Songs

Jesus in Worship and Wonder: OUT 2017
Melody, Mystery and the Messiah   Psalms
978-0-9933445-9-6

Jesus in the Major Prophets:
Incarnation, Crucifixion, Resurrection and Ascension
Isaiah – Daniel

Jesus in the Minor Prophets:
Revealing the Plans of God
Hosea – Malachi

Jesus in Exile and Return:
Creating a Space for Grace
Ezra – Esther + input from the prophets

Jesus in the Silent Years:
Providence in the Wait for The Messiah
End of the Old Testament to start of the Gospels